Where The Wild Things Were

By Susan Goldsworthy OLY & Sydney Goldsworthy, illustrated by Sydney Goldsworthy

Chemin de Bellerive 23
P.O. Box 915
CH – 1001 Lausanne
Switzerland
Tel: +41 21 618 01 11 – Fax: +41 21 618 07 07
www.imd.org

Typeset in Felt Tip Roman created by Mark Simonson Studio and Gabriel Sans ™ by Fontfabric.

ISBN Print: 978-2-940485-28-4
ISBN EPUB: 978-2-940485-29-1
Designed by Yves Balibouse, BBH Solutions Visuelles, Vevey, Switzerland, www.bbhgraphic.com.
Printed by IngramSpark.

Set sometime, not so far away, in the future

Tell me a bedtime story Grandma?
About what you did when you were my age?

When I was your age...

I ate with aardvarks

I boogied with bears

I chilled with chimpanzees

I dabbled with deer

I engaged with elephants

I frolicked with foxes

I giggled with gorillas

I hid with hedgehogs

I idled with iguanas

I jostled with jaguars

I knuckled with kangaroos

I lolloped with lions

I mingled with macaws

I nosedived with narwhals

I ogled with owls

I painted with pangolins

I quibbled with quails

I ran with rhinoceros

I swam with sea lions

I traded with tigers

I umpired with uakaris

I visited with vipers

I woke up with wolves

I (e)xplored with Xantus's hummingbirds

I yodeled with yaks

And I zealously zigzagged with zebras

I want to dabble and jostle and lollop and yodel!

Oh, pretty please will you take me along, Grandma?

I would, my Little Dove, but they lived in the wild, and the wild is no more.
The wild? What's that?

A place where creatures roamed free, that's where they used to be.
And where did they all go?

They had to go away...

There was no room left for them to stay...

What did you do Grandma? Once your friends could no longer play?

I wrote this book for you, I wrote this book to say:

what did we do once we knew

That the animals were going away?

We built them vast natural reserves,

We built them a big beautiful bay,

We gave them what all life deserves

We gave them time and space to be,
and we started to live in harmony

Because that was the only way,
to make sure they'd come back someday

Goodnight Little Dove

Goodnight Grandma

I hope they can come back to stay

The End

What did we do once we knew?

Imagine a planet without dolphins? Without elephants, without lions, without tigers, without whales? We are fast headed towards a world where that will be a fact. And along with the extinction of other creatures, we must now face the possibility of our own extinction too.

On October 30th 2018, the media reported on the release of the WWF's Living Planet Report, a comprehensive study of trends in global biodiversity and the health of the planet that is based on the Living Planet Index from The Royal Zoological Society. One key statistic shared was that, in less than 50 years, we've seen an overall decline of 60% in population sizes of vertebrate species.

"This is far more than just being about losing the wonders of nature, desperately sad though that is," said Mike Barrett, executive director of science and conservation at WWF UK. *"This is actually now jeopardising the future of people. Nature is not a 'nice to have' – it is our life-support system."*

To ensure that the other species that inhabit our earth can survive and thrive, they need to have space. Experts say that, as of 2018, almost 15% of the Earth's land surface and just over 7% of the world's oceans are formally protected and that this needs to increase to 30% by 2030 and 50% by 2050. Today, only 4% of the world's mammals are wild. The other 96% are livestock, domestic animals and humans.

As with any major change, there appears to be three ways in which people are responding to the daily news about the looming collapse of civilization as we know it; Denial, Distraction and Despair. With Denial, it is too difficult to face or accept and so, instead, we dismiss it and ignore the facts. With Distraction, we accept the situation but find it overwhelming and so seek refuge in the continuation of our day-to-day lives, tranquilized by the trivial, with small adjustments here and there. And then there is Despair, where people face the facts head on and then feel paralyzed or hopeless as they are confronted by the enormity of the loss in front of us.

However, a fourth way is to engage in Dialogue: to converse with each other to raise awareness and prompt action that can engender a sense of 'functional hope' about what can be done. How can leaders act with responsibility to create space for participatory dialogue where hope can flourish and decisive action be taken? How can we, collectively, challenge what is and inspire what could be?

The 2030 Agenda for Sustainable Development, adopted by all United Nations member states in 2015, provides a shared blueprint for peace and prosperity for people and the planet, now and into the future. At its heart are the 17 Sustainable Development Goals (SDGs), which are an urgent call for action by all countries – developed and developing - in a global partnership. They recognize that ending poverty and other deprivations must go hand-in-hand with strategies that improve health and education, reduce inequality and spur economic growth – all while tackling climate change and working to preserve our oceans and forests. SDG 17 calls for partnership for the goals as it is vital that we work together to meet the enormity of the challenge facing us. Businesses must work with NGOs, with governments, across countries and communities. Together, we can achieve more.

Susan has previously co-authored two award-winning business books, *Care to Dare* and *Choosing Change*, and, ironically, both these titles provide vital messages for humanity given the current world context. We must now consciously choose to change and both dare and care at a societal level; Dare to push for new technological solutions, new approaches to the way we do business, to our economic and societal models, and Care to look after what we can before it is too late. We must remember what it is we love about the natural world, and then do our utmost to preserve it. We must accept what we must let go of in our current ways of living to make the changes necessary and to work together in partnership to use our ingenuity as a force for good.

As a member of IMD's faculty, Susan has the privilege of working with executives and discussing leadership and change at the individual, team, organizational and societal levels. When talking about the current world context, executives share that it is often our youth who are influencing the older generations – our children and grandchildren who hold us to account for what is happening to nature and life in this Age of the Anthropocene.

As a writer, storyteller and artist, Sydney is passionate about the need to raise awareness and appreciation for all creatures. She strives to capture the essence of every animal she paints and to write in a way that invokes an array of emotions in the reader.

There is a line in the poem 'Hieroglyphic Stairway' by Drew Dellinger that asks, "What did you do once you knew?" So, we asked ourselves, now we know, what will we do? This prompted us to create this storybook, Where the Wild Things Were, dedicated to all of us, our children and our children's children and to all the species that co-exist on this rather special and unique place called Earth. We aim to express our care, to bear witness to the wonder in our world and to express the need for responsible leadership to protect what we still can before it is too late.

We both hope that you enjoy this book and feel moved to act in whatever way, big or small, to make an impact for the better in our more-than-human world.

A percentage of the sales from this book will go to charities supporting the protection of wildlife.

Resources & References

View the Living Planet Report at the following link: http://wwf.panda.org/knowledge_hub/all_publications/living_planet_report_2018/

Find out more about biodiversity loss and the role business can play at: http://wwf.panda.org/get_involved/partner_with_wwf/corporate_partnerships/.

Find out more about the UN Sustainable Development Goals (SDGs) at: https://sustainabledevelopment.un.org/?menu=1300

Find out more about knowledge on climate change at: https://www.ipcc.ch/reports/

Read about biodiversity loss and protection at: https://www.nationalgeographic.com/environment/2019/01/conservation-groups-call-for-protecting-30-percent-earth-2030/

Find out more about the IMD CLEAR Senior Executive Program at: https://www.imd.org/clear/leadership-transformation/

Find out more about the Climate Reality Project at: https://www.climaterealityproject.org/

Hear Drew Dellinger read Hieroglyphic Stairway at: https://www.youtube.com/watch?v=XW63UUthwSg

Find eco-conscious news, writing, art & poetry at: https://www.onceweknew.com/

Biographies

Susan Goldsworthy OLY
Co-author

A former Olympic finalist, European & Commonwealth medalist, life-long vegan and award-winning writer, Susan is passionate about working with others to turn knowledge into behavior. Affiliate Professor of Leadership & Organizational Change at IMD Business School, she is co-author of the award-winning books *Care to Dare* and *Choosing Change*, associate director of IMD senior leadership program, CLEAR and codirector of Skolkovo Business School & IMD leadership program, LIFT.

Susan has more than 20 years' senior management experience in large multinationals and, for more than a decade, has run her own company focusing on leadership development, change communications and executive coaching.

For her Doctorate in Organizational Change with Hult Ashridge Business School, Susan has been researching the role of Hope in the current world context. She holds a Masters degree (MSc) in Consulting and Coaching for Change with HEC and Oxford University, an Executive Masters in the Neuroscience of Leadership, and certification in Coaching for Leadership & Professional Development with The Tavistock Institute. She is qualified in numerous psychometric assessments and is a Climate Reality Leader.

It is her hope that by cutting through Denial, Distraction and Despair, we can cultivate a desire for Dialogue about how best to protect what we still can of this magical more-than-human world.

Sydney Goldsworthy
Co-author and Illustrator

Sydney runs GoldsWoof where she creates various stylistic, colorful and abstract portraits of a myriad of subjects. A story-teller at heart, she has always valued each medium for its capacity to evoke emotions and convey meaning.

Raised vegetarian and surrounded by animals, she has always had a sensitive heart, caring deeply for the living creatures all around us. Through her art she hopes to raise awareness and appreciation for endangered species as well as life in its many wonderful forms. Sydney loves to learn about our world and she hopes she might be able to educate others by communicating what she discovers.

Influenced by cosmology, mythology, fantasy, science and philosophy, her belief is that we must strive to be compassionate, aiming to help one another to grow. With open hearts and minds we can achieve harmony and balance. Let us steer our world towards a brighter, more sustainable future, the only way we can: together.

REAL LEARNING. REAL IMPACT

At IMD, we develop leaders who transform organizations and contribute to society. We are an independent academic institution with Swiss roots and global reach, established by business leaders for business leaders.

Led by an expert and diverse faculty, we deliver Real Learning Real Impact through a unique combination of teaching, research, coaching and advisory services. Challenging what is and inspiring what could be, we are the trusted learning partner of choice for ambitious individuals and organizations.

Based in Lausanne (Switzerland) and Singapore, IMD has been ranked in the top five for executive education worldwide for 15 years and in the top three for the last eight years (*Financial Times*). IMD is the only Swiss business school and one of less than hundred globally to hold the coveted "triple crown" of accreditations from AACSB, EFMD EQUIS and AMBA, the gold standard for global best practice.

CPSIA information can be obtained
at www.ICGtesting.com
Printed in the USA
LVIC061149071019
633397LV00015B/468

* 9 7 8 2 9 4 0 4 8 5 2 8 4 *